BIRD CONJURING

Also by David Cloutier

Poetry
Garrapata
Soft Lightnings
Tongue and Thunder
Ghost Call
Tracks of the Dead

Translations and Versions
By the Stream of Antique Song: Oral Poems
The Waters of Uliassutai: Mongol Songs
News of Love: Poems by Hafiz
The Beaches of Thule: Poems by Jean Laude
Transparent God: Poem sequence by Claude Esteban
Spirit Spirit: Shaman Songs
My Grandfather's House: Tlingit Songs
White Road: Selected Poems by Claude Esteban
Northwest Coast Songs
The Ear of the Bull: Nine French Poets (with Stephen Coon) editor

SUNSTONE
PRESS

BIRD CONJURING
Poems
(1971–2021)

DAVID CLOUTIER

SUNSTONE
PRESS

SANTA FE

Sunstone books may be purchased for educational, business, or sales promotional use.
For information please write: Special Markets Department, Sunstone Press,
P.O. Box 2321, Santa Fe, New Mexico 87504-2321.
Printed on acid-free paper
eBook 978-1-61139-415-3

Library of Congress Cataloging-in-Publication Data

Names: Cloutier, David, author.
Title: Bird conjuring : poems (1971-2021) / by David Cloutier.
Description: Santa Fe : Sunstone Press, [2022] | Summary: "A collection of
  poems by a well known Southwestern US poet"-- Provided by publisher.
Identifiers: LCCN 2022019586 | ISBN 9781632933676 (paperback) | ISBN
  9781611394153 (epub)
Subjects: LCGFT: Poetry.
Classification: LCC PS3553.L66 B57 2022 | DDC 811/.54--dc23/eng/20220520
LC record available at https://lccn.loc.gov/2022019586

WWW.SUNSTONEPRESS.COM
SUNSTONE PRESS / POST OFFICE BOX 2321 / SANTA FE, NM 87504-2321 /USA
(505) 988-4418

BIRD CONJURING
for Carolyn

Many of the poems, some in different versions, appeared in:

Akwesasne Notes, Antioch Anecdotes, Arion's Dolphin, The Arts Journal, Aspect, Aspect Anthology, The Blacksmith, Blue Cloud Quarterly, California Quarterly, Cardinal, A Carolina Literary Companion, Chelsea, Cincinnati Poetry Review, Dakotah Territory, Decade, A Glass of Green Tea with Edwin Honig, Hawaii Pacific Review, Hellcoal Annual, Invisible City, Ironwood, Ishmael, Karamu, Kumanitu, Lapis Lazuli, Mundus Artium, Nedge, New Age, Northeast Journal, Pembroke Magazine, Prism international (Canada), *Raccoon, River Styx, Roanoke Roots, Sanskrit, Shaman, Stinktree, Tree, Trickster, Two Xmas Poems, The Wayah Review, Wip (Works in progress), The Woly of Swot* (UK), and *The Works.* Heartfelt thanks to each editor.

Also, in these books and chapbooks: *Garrapata (tel-let 44, 1995), Soft Lightnings* (Copper Beech Press, 1982), *Tongue and Thunder* (Copper Beech Press, 1980), *Tracks of the Dead* (Blue Cloud Chapbook #3, 1976) and *Ghost Call* (Copper Beech Press, 1976). Deep gratitude to editors Edwin Honig, John Martone and Benet Tvedten, OSB.

"Martyr of Baghdad" was included in *Love in a Time of War,* a multi-media production by Jump-Start, San Antonio, 2008. Gracias! Sandra Dunn.

Cover: Adam Fuss, Unique Ciba Chrome photogram from the series "In Between."

Other acknowledgements noted within.

CONTENTS

I.
ANOTHER TIME

II.
TRACKS OF THE DEAD

III.
OTHER LIGHTS

And there is another bird
that raises
one wing on the outside
and the other inside
—Roberto Juarroz

FOREWORD

Where is wherever
we can go
        "Migrant Words"

Word-alchemist, David Cloutier is the *Bird Conjuring,* using the gifts left to him by his Irish/Breton ancestors: story-telling, bard-songs, heart-murmurs, eye-lightning. This is a vision-quest, a quest for vision. David Cloutier walks out of the Garden without a map, sharing his harvest of story, poem, myth from the mulch of drumming voices of the Algonquin, the sound of sand rubbing Point Pinos, answering the riddles of wolf and lion. *Bird Conjuring* is a life-time of walking with dreamers, seers, in-and-out and beyond the mirror.

In what night or song
rises this dream
        "Griffin"

There is wisdom, beauty, flight and light here, *Bird Conjuring* is sacred territory. David Cloutier gives us voices of the ear-of-the-heart. He calls the spirits home from Konya, Garrapata, Nepenthe, Fez, Cardona to rest here. David Cloutier holds the reins of a lifetime of archives he lives while letting the reins drop into his fertilized nursery of images and dreams, where poems are born, nourished and shared. David has his own time machine: you are invited in.

With the tongue asleep
the heart wakes
        "Mute Song"

    —James McGrath, poet of *At the Edgelessness of Light, Mixed Greens, A Temporary Silence,* and other books from Sunstone Press.

I.

ANOTHER TIME

ANOTHER TIME

Let's start again
go
rename the constellations

blue lightning chair   winged reindeer
harvest of living jewels

white moth echoes
signature of the dark ones   fistful of polished stones

triangle of burning breath
daughter of copper filings   mother's misplaced spoons

EACH NIGHT
for Hugo Leckey

When darkness climbs
a one-eyed navigator
up from the broken coast
we shake out the bones
blow dust off the compass
and drift

'There is a Light that
Fails in My Mouth'
Georg Trakl

It comes in the rumbling
like the night train

in the dark coughing clouds
flash it comes

a light caught on a pinpoint
an entire legacy

like the bright numerals left
from a house fork-struck

it comes in each drop it drops
down the chimney

comes in the wind it swings
round the vane

silent glowing in the rain
like love

it comes like a season I never thought
would come

EASTER EVENING
THE WORLD IS FULL
OF RESURRECTIONS

Even the locks are gone
from their doors
they fly away

the coats of night
drop from my shoulders
the dark cap is not on my head

Luna waves her sleeves
illumines this table like grace
a feast

I rise and strike a match
a blue finger draws out
the wooden light

and fills the room
with bent shadows
blind paupers

we converse
all night and drink
in silence

outside the roundest
moon of the season
above the rooftops a bright eye floats

THE FISH-RIBBED ARC
THE NIGHT

And lit the high grandfather hair

down here rooftops and rooftops
and dark
men reap darkness

they pack it away
mouths agape
gray sacks gold-clipped
tight

once light opened
they drew off past
yawned skies threadbare

I lost them

ASLEEP AWAKE
for Anne

You never hinder
that triangle of feathers
as it passes through your rooms

you never question
those holy animals
adrift in an ark of dream

nor the luminous hand
that moves under
each water

it's true
every star's an angel

galaxies silently whirl
beneath your forehead's
newest moon

DROUGHT

Three months
not even a cloud
yet buckets were set
on stoops each night
like rows of beggar tins

stars do not turn on their faces
their hollows are black holes
in the dark

the eyes of the thirsty
turn in their sockets
without tears
against the sky their fists
unroll ten radial signs

chimneys of prayer rise
up like hopes
nibbling the horizon
aerial cattle float

INTO THE NIGHT

I ask all the questions
they roll off my tongue
stones
blotched chipped gifts
laid out like prairie towns
before the sky's broad answerless
question

tonight
the stars are both the teeth and the wounds

my hands fold on the dark table
blue shaking
stars
or paupers kneeling into nothing
mumbling
zeros

Broken Water
   Frozen Light
                in memory, Paul Celan (1920–1970)

*Deep
in the time-crevasse
by the
honeycomb-ice,
there waits, as a breath crystal,
your unimpeachable
testimony.*

    *

A tongue
circumambulates the night
same night you
swallowed whole it swallowed
you in belly embrace
breaking you down to its own
bare filaments lit
you lived

    *

Town wounded into evening
gray dream
a shredded poster
catcalls
and dense water
the salt of everything
close by
a cracked window

your hand swims the railing
tin mug a lead shadow
things we oil we take with us
they stay
on the surface lids quivering
and below
wave rising
your heart a boat
in the grain

*

The old-life spindle spun
out in your ear
gods' horn
ravenswan came
a flesh drum beating
away the green
the wood
the deepest ring
a leap in the skull's wide tent
or up your coiled lamp
another world
a tree with nine nests
charred twig in the tenth
spark
firelights go migrating through your dark

*

Was it the dark of your mother's
mother's prayer
the dark of your mother's mouth
held off
in the farthest iron-there
or
was it the white of your father's
memory-hair

a higher bright than any
metalshine ever
shone here

*

An Eye
followed you
a subtracted sun
moon
eye Adonai
a flame eye
spun on its stick
rain Eye
churning
consuming each sign
the wax night
its own smudged light
a fierce One

*

Dirt-feather
air-feather
lodged between
blades the frozen leaves
you who lived
deep between them
with that shaft of pale light
overhead a thin knife
you could never forget
*Those-of-the Name-and-Its-
Round-Abyss*

*

Black drops to black
sleep
black froths to black

bubbles
gods that are dead
in No-one's Name
black bubbles blank
moons
disappear in river spirals
an impaled light your star
breaks free
lamps blink along the rim
black gush swilled gutters
cathedrals stagger
toward the edge

a tear rolls back into its eye
a drum

a tree-
high thought
strikes the note of light: there are
still songs to sing beyond
mankind.

Italics: words of Paul Celan

Homing

Between star and snow
you'll nail down a roof
and the mantis and the moth
will faint beneath the leaves
as the hour and its whiteness
curls into their shells
you learn to see in the dark
this is the month the ice twirls a knife
and scrapes its names on your heart
your blindness hair
your deepest purple shadow
those scars you call your hands
they alone can help you this time
forget the match the wick

Red Dream Circle
a stitch in time saves nine

One time one
stitch
the heart sewn by hand

this time torn
cloth
sew nine thin lines

*

One's drawn through the eye
two bound   a red-gold thread
a bundle of blood's the third
full twist at the curve stitch   four winds entwine
a sky that holds all   a seamless palm
five fingers drift
beyond   six is the flex of the thought of return
it climbs above itself a seventh arm
eight is the blink that doubles the fourth
drawn through the loop to the place where thimbles
rise   nine veins thread one dawn-spun eye

Unseen
each slate breaks
off the roof

unshattered we lie in the snow

ah that a god could be
spun in straw
a wheel sewn in flesh

this wick not consumed

night sprinkled in blood
each star a drop
a shine

rising
a wing in stone

Aureole

Egg of light
the bright ones
play round

viols and pipes
crumhorns
timbrels lutes
drums

her face illumined
albumen
rides a crescent
crowned

and the yolk
of that longing
strikes a bell

after a painting by Sint Jans (15 c.)

STRING OF WELLS

Door
black hole
that opens down

whose house
I can't see
your face

your night
a paw crossing
the eyes

your tongues
lapping up
my sleep

*

I dare
sunken jar
to name you

woman
root of breath
plunge

hem unraveling
at the threshold
don't leave me

tears rise
our levels
both drop

*

Virgin eyes
overgrown
I forget her

unveil
the blue windows
one after one

uncover
uncover
pull the lids aside

beneath each
stone
blind sky

*

Abyss to abyss
you give
yourself away

you wake
under everyone's
tongue

clouds see
themselves taste
their own flesh

each passed through
your circle
once

*

All day at the ropes
bucket
bucket

suns hauled
shaking
out of the ground

poured into
a black trough
splashed over flanks

I lower
my eyes
I drink

*

We meet
there's a table
greater than ourselves

I break my old hands
you show me
water

a center of circles
I see
another face

anchor
aglow
my deep one

MOUNTAIN

Sometimes if you turn
you can see a white mountain
hovering transparent
over your shoulder
if it's clear you can see
pale wings circling
that long-eared peak
and there just below
slopes of stone roses
this can happen
even if your feet
have long worn to sand
and you came all this way
with your hands dripping salt
as if turning back was an ocean

Poverty

So you pass through
darks

you pass through
mountains

the only way to go
they say

cave in the center
root of the peak

on the road under stones
me dancing

Becoming

In the clear wind of an autumn night
I whistle beneath the pines
this is one way I free myself
like the lake that takes the face of the moon
I become one note

TING

Shape of what
went beyond before

sky-wound
hand-wound

overturned vessel
spilt sun

what remains
holy shards

what remains
some splintered wood

what will come
a little fire

a thousand quick arms
to grow

mold something
to raise

a vessel jade
handles eyes

ears smooth
rings hold

a circle to receive
sky

circle to feed
new tongue

Ting: an ancient Chinese ceremonial vessel; a hexagram of the I Ching.

A Clearing

This slow emptying
like a cup
that's the sky

even white clouds
whirl away

events poised within
stilled content
an opening of palms

you would say
this is another
place but

a clear stone glides
through pure water

ORPHAN SONG

Up there where branch-tips fan
like the bones in wings
and the blue air pulses and pulses
in that place too I was born

MOON SONGS

To stretch a skin over the entire sky
and thump and thump out light

*

This drum
overturned

a lake
the dead rise from

raining
toward another hill

*

Beneath the thistle
a wing-blade whitening

beside the path
a pebble swells

and here a shell half
filled with water

quivering
quivering

to the call

*

If the ear's a drum
it is a bowl of water

if something's lost
a fish swims there

in each mouth we catch
a moon-coin rising

over nets
on the other shore

LAKE OF THE SUN

Level on level
bright jars going up

to the zenith
where the yellow
chair shines

this is how
water speaks
with the sky

as far as the eye
pierces miles

Arrow

Days of air
speechless
blind noons arcing
higher

the arrow

voice taut
and the target invisible
water

long aim of song

and the vowel being
chipped
into a cloud

string-throb

tongue and thunder

ASCENDANT

From here this
hill the voice
climbed

you can speak
that wound beyond
the scorpion's thorn

the skull halved
and voiceless
out in the still

from here
you can invent
the wheel

Thirst

In the thicket
deerstep and shadow

the echo instant
leaps beyond

silence
and the water beaming

drink the moon
dark

Poem on the Slopes

Storm that scatters the calendar
wind unhinging the hours

we were walking in the twilight
on a slope of muteness
each step a wounding stone

to go on
is the ground that bears us up
to go on

take a stick
a thorn imagines flowers
and your need *charm of the bright hand*

distill thunder a mantra
shifting winds can erase the paths

The Middle Way

Sky pouring over
earth
tendrils trembling

ferns and stems
the wild rose leaves
drink in song

this is the path
'the middle way'

what levels the peaks
lifts the deserts
home

ACQUIRER OF THE ALPHABET

Oracle twigs to the sky
uplifted

notch and slash
the lightning script
emblazoned across the night

hand haloed by starlight
all tongues praise you

who bore to the earth
the voice that moves
through marks

THE LONG CHASE

Alive
on the earth's arc
clear
triumph of horizons

meshed with the wind
twisting a path
through fields of neighs
and bells

and here
a bright hoofprint
now the long chase
starts again

to race toward the east
without bridle
to harness
far horse of solitude

GRIFFIN

In what night or song
rises this dream

what sky

where falcon and lion tear
through each other

light into darkness
to one

bright ferocity of distance
in an old name

this *griffin*

roaring
through a beak of dawn

With the tongue asleep
the heart wakes

elder tongue
king of vowels

in the quiet
shining

inside
a mammal's head

our rising
dumbness

nods

TOWARD THE EQUINOX

Whirl that's a stillness
at the center of the world

day and dark
on the scales

wide heart

*   *   *

Immaculate

the pale gorge
the day but
deep

cove smoking
stones brimming
own stillness

little voice
the mosses
call out

shadow
shadow

beneath last night's
lightninged
trunk

a root that's
still bright

who could contain it

the sun filling
up the blue jug
mouth

East

*   *   *

*Egg of air
egg of fire
egg of soil
egg of tears*

        *

Light breaking
from the heart
and the sky tonight

an oval that opens it all

there are wells
there are hands
lifting their darks

mirrors beyond the snow

*   *   *

Morning
a wagon of lamps

reined up
full spectrum of blues

this they'll never see
in the city

even underground
it's raining

*   *   *

Night has a hand
it would burn any face

a flame far beyond
any shine

night hides its
skull of quicksilver

a clear jar filled
with cinnabar
moans

o
white star
red star

dark is your
love
o

*   *   *

Up to crown
the stone thrust
out

bright one climbing
home

the air is a basket of voices

light and its echo

a whisper of ash
swirls
into vertical choirs

a singular fire
lifting the lungs

everything
is sung

*   *   *

Sun and moon
wear the same face

this the crocus told

II.

TRACKS OF THE DEAD

FOR JAMES SCHEVILL

Tracks of the Dead

Fog swirls
look deep beneath
your own face

the ancestors
migrate between
the broken hills

by their eyes smokeless
fires you can trace
the sunken path

the spiral
treading back
toward new worlds

Cedar

In this place
the heart's tree
is surely
cedar

where blood
climbs
the wood must
be red

here silence
owns a voice
pure hum
no echo

just scent
rising up
a hundred lives
rings ring

MOON OF BLINDING SNOW
for the Oglala Lakota, Wounded Knee

There where feminine
blood and child
blood spilled
voices swirl
up from the ground

drawn by the Moon
of Blinding Snow
blood-rivers widen
waters uplifting
the heart

ice breaks up
bones are sprouting
marrow-roots feed
those who stand
there like the living fists
of the dead sprung
up from this wounded ground

flesh and bone
flowers rise
and open like the eyes
of a living planet
see

THROUGH A WORN SMOOTH FACE
for Kevin

timber
darker
timber

*

It's slow work
retooling the familiar

features
hewn out inside

lone trunk
a buried wick

a sleep
encircling sleep

pith rustling
to be lit

whole face

Dream a New Death
for Edwin Honig

Beyond the fences
you begin to reach
this dark you wake
outside yourself

as if that dream
you rode to birth
a beast with eight legs
lifted its huge head

and passed behind
as you tracked your fire
a lone torch chasing south
it tracks your dark

that dream a face
a storm of bells
snow glacial breath
a massive whiteness

falls you flow
toward your center
flung round your neck
a wreath of wordless song

a cloud treads empty air
an animal stillness
licks your ear
you're gone

your bones glow
the same light as moss
your newborn waking head
a living stone of living stones

on your outstretched tongue
that ridge of dark
an amber triangle
quartz flares up

Glyph

Down the deertrack
comes flying
a spirit afire

all pulsating
oval
an egg or eye

yet flying
Sky-lit-bright-hair-behind

and those who see
came to this
smooth rock face

to chip at once
the raised limbs'
amazement

in heart
in stone

MESSAGE FROM THE OLD
    DEITIES

Though we vanished
from memory
like ice under flame

ash and oak
all the long groves
razed

we revolve the world
still

Raven's Boast

Fan of knives
I can cut
any air

I know my
blade
I can shine

I know dark
water am a dark
water

light-thief
eater
I'm my name

inside my eye
rolling up
over there

that moon
caw-haw
seed

NEW MOON

All night this
mouth without a tongue
call in the songman
let us rounding
glow

POST CARD, KING PHILIP MONUMENT
(CIRCA 1910)

GHOST CALL

I

Call or a hand
moving over this ground
hunting again new skins
this time the awl
is passing unseen
through nails
through tables dark wood
speech

hand or a call
going low over this town
to sew at last
its early light
within to glint
between

for things to light up
look out on us
rocks their scattered depths

air
water
the blue head
to open us

to raise on our elbows
the pigeon's dream

to grow back into itself
hear its own cry
low over shallows
dwarf pines
ferns
seed

now windows now twirling
in their clearest molecules
bedposts and kettles
doorknobs gleam

a man and a woman
say *yes* in their sleep

*   *   *   *

There are nights when the stars
pulse without a sound

drums
to wake the cobbles
fill the potholes with sudden light

there are nights when the sky
wears a silver tail and a tongue
that points in all directions

lamps doze in their coils
doorways grow deeper
no one is seen

yet in sleep
there's a night and a river
and a bay

a fish that moves nameless
as the sky's real name

*   *   *   *

Call call
call in another tongue
call of entwined reeds

comes in its voice
an emblem of dust
of bone
the moon's drenched beak

I crawl out of my skin
like quartz from a hill

I'm molding a tongue
maize-gold

set in this night
in a pouch of mud

it grows
it glows

II

I fall down
my throat
to speak you

You of this Place

I fall
down my ear
to hear you

breaking yourself
underground

there were nights
when they bled
from their hands
in the swamps

covered their eyes
with their own
leaping blood

just to glimpse
your thighs of bark

your stag ears
under branches

your snout
bright snout
piercing the surface
My Speaking Blue Fish

now come
come back
and you can
now

as radiator
basket
cup glove rug

I fall down
my eye
to see you

You of this Place

between You

    *   *   *   *

I'll walk the old names
I'll walk the old names
in a tongue that never
named you

I'll walk the old names
toward a shadowed face
I'll walk the old names
toward new words

    *   *   *   *

White
over algae
oyster
pale fin

wing of the gull
foam
chalk wave

Kichtan
I speak you
I move close
you change

a drip of light
between the briars
the startled maple skin

up above
in the shadow
in the crow's shape
he preens the darkest wing

Hobbamocko
I say you
in the crow's shape
Hobbamocko

beak of nightcalls
chest of thunders
three nailed talon
of waking lightnings

speak me
Hobbamocko
eye full of clearest evenings

* * * *

Hobbomocko's Songs

Arrow in my leg
my blood riding
over this world
from now on
every day will know
its dark

   *

My claws hooked
in the throat
of a cloud

I rip loose

rain
rain
till dawn

   *

I die my own
death
in the pounding
breast of a hare

I see myself
squirming toward a hole
under stone

while overhead
fear my own
life
spirals down

   *

The other one who tore
me out of his skull

gave me pain

this bag of teeth
this beak I wear

I nest beneath his skin
that other one

bright other one
I am
I am

       *   *   *   *

You say
you are him
he is you
you are your brother
Kichtan

wing under leaf
Hobbamocko
takes a shell of day
to see his eye in

wing over water
Kichtan
takes a wooden shadow
to see each thing

Kichtan
Hobbamocko

both the bill that sweeps
the shallows
the hairy salt worm

*   *   *   *

Now come
come back
and you can
now

as radiator
basket
all the small things

I fall down
my ear
to hear you

breaking yourself
underground

III

Little goose of balsa
painted green
swings round on its stick
in the rain

if you listen
to it rattle
it sings

if you listen
to it spins
it prays

*   *   *   *

When was it
that we all forgot
how to make them

the wooden ones
anymore

those hewn of night
those hewn of light

how we needed them
how we need them
how

when our hands
grew so thick
with the useful

that the small tools
flint knife bone awl
dropped through
three dozen centuries
to shatter the tiles
on the eleventh floor

when was it that
we forgot how
to lay in the tiny
eyes of shell
tie around cedar necks
strings of bark
praying knots
moon of iron
or copper moons

to sing into them
sing into them
all our lungs' roots
vowels to beg
new songs

when was it we
even forgot how
to fall out of ourselves
into a stone
the twig's slice of blue
over the snow
or the line where every wave
gives up to sand

it was when
our heads climbed
over the necks
tried to cast off
their earth-shaped skulls

and it wasn't toward the sky

it wasn't toward the sky

but to forget the blood
in little beads of lead

*   *   *   *

They bit their tongues
in order to forget
smudged ashen crosses
on their foreheads to forget
what's the real what
of two paths that meet

they went out to look
for clean blood
on their fists
to forget
that She's the one
the One is she

the trail that crosses trail
both worlds

*   *   *   *

Here she is here
she is
the Little Sybil
the last one
first of the nine seeing sisters

she's the one
who eats the hearts of things

'She was dressed like this: she wore a blue mantle fastened with
straps and adorned with stones all the way to the hem. She had a
necklace of glass beads. On her head she wore a black lambskin
hood lined with white cat's fur. She carried a staff with a brass-

bound knob studded with stones. She wore a belt made of
touchwood, from which hung a large pouch and in this she
kept the charms....'

there she is there
she is
the Little Sybil
the last one
first of the nine seeing sisters

and this is what she ate

'She was given a gruel made from goat's milk, and a main dish
of hearts from the various kinds of animals…she used a brass
spoon, and a knife with a walrus-tusk handle bound with rings
of copper; the blade had a broken point.'

      *   *   *   *

The Little Sybil's Song

I swam to the glowing
house beneath the lake

I'm the one
who walks the meadow
from there to here

I wake in your sickle
I sleep in the grain

I'm the one
who knows the secret
of dung and plough

I've lost myself
in the udders of your cattle

I grow wide
in your pupils
I grow so small

I'm the little yellow
tongue of the sky

beneath my dress
I carry every child
in a sack of mud that glows

*   *   *   *

She's the one
who ate the hearts of things

*   *   *   *

She fell under their hands
hands full of flames and snakes

only the children could save her
with their tongues

moon and star

the tongues of children

woman who fills the sky

she fell under their hands
hands filled with snakes and flames

only the tongues of children
save her

moon and star

woman who fills the sky

in tiny skulls
all lit

goose-rider

    *   *   *   *

Little goose of balsa
painted green
swings round on its stick
in the rain

if you listen
to it rattle
it sings

if you listen
to it spin
it prays

IV

Tap with a worm-hewn
root to wake
metals cast into embarrassed rods
hills powdered and squared
into angular zeros

myself asleep in my sleep
and the world's

track the beast
who stalks
who diminishes the horizon
dwelling inside a glove of humiliated tars

crawl back into the shadow
beg forgiveness from the small

for both ears to come to life
under this helmet of engines
hear the secret compassion
metal calling home to metal

the night that grows invisible
trains wincing under stars

*   *   *   *

Often in sleep you can touch
the retreating heart of the sky
or dive below the surface
toward the drumming wrist of this place
where hair twines around the body

and ribs glow inside
where the wolf leaves traces with his nails
and deer graze down beneath pines
that crumbled into themselves
five hundred years ago

further on there's always
someone whispering
into flame into a stone
who listens with an ear
held up to pouring water
who listens
listens
earthworms turning among pebbles
each dragonfly's four wings
at once

*   *   *   *

We call after you
with cloth mouths
we carry your losses
around on our shoulders

we drive back at dusk
by a lone block of stone
call you out of your hut
behind water

has the bridge been extinguished
has the grass forgot your prints

does your face still hold
its light behind
your death

(Metacomet's Prophecy)

Something's rising
billions the living
things long gone

wave high wave
roll the night
of this ground

grave of the real man
dragonfly wings the beak
turned in to the sand

his song
something's rising
hold on

the weight of this greenness
quakes in his shoulder
brooding elbow

earth will shrug
something's rising
dream

the dream of last time
he flings the blank
mask we oh wove oh

Animal Riddles

(Crow)

Caw over the day
night's eyes raising
                    a roost in the blueness

peak of a fir
lifting away into the four
spaces

                open
the feathered layers
sky's bundle

                pure
                dark

        *   *   *   *

(Goose)

One whose skin is the shadow of water

fog and its hands
dream reeds

                there's one
                rising over

the house of bending rains

voice that's a wing
                    changing into a cloud

to nest by the moon's brimming tongue

        *   *   *   *

(WOLF)

King iron atop the rocks overviewing
            the lake
King gray with his furs of fog

                there's an eye that struggles
                with the air's thousand lights

                there's an eye staring
                out of the ground

        King paw between the hills
                ten abandoned villages

        the only scent which no scent

                moss and stone

        *   *   *   *

(DRAGONFLY)

Noon always buzzing
an eye has ten thousand windows

green loop over
a pool in the woods
                        even sun

                    tied in

green medicine

veins of lightning seen
transparent wings

                    arcings

        *   *   *   *

(FROG)

Dark calling out of a living chest
wish for the air
                    wings and lights

what is it
            moon
            or a pond
            that makes the throat
                    move

deepest rising
out that joins

all song

        *   *   *   *

(LION)

            Born in the storm
                over up and down

mane flaming spirit
                        brother
                        blood
guide through the woods

all fours
          dark
                dark always
   lit to the left

a roar windy cave
rearing up on hind legs

                              dawn tail
                              fire banner
                              mammal sky

          *   *   *   *

(*Reindeer*)

               When dark breaks out
in roots of branching
     bone

               you can dip
               your hoof
               in the center

bright stream

               *

A gust of light rides over the roofs

who owns the sky's night eyes

     winged one

belled one
four-legged
clear one

*   *   *   *

(*FISH*)

Even at the source of water
tail always shifting
scales flashing

         meteors
mirrors

either side
a pebble gleaming

         lidless
         egg of sparks
seeing

     out and farther inward

fiery current
swirls deeper

holy diving

       fin on fin

Incantations Over Water
for Karoniaktatie

Fishwings
fishwings

come to me

and you moon
old worked bone

with your light

you night you
abalone eyes

*

No luck
for days then

this dream

net draws up
a living rock

*

Bright tail
swirls

deep water

skeletal o flung
spray

soak me

                    *

Let this one
go

wing over water

gravel sand coast
a sudden oyster

and this one

small tongue
in a beak

                    *

Then rise
to the rim

there are islands

all gulls
ice ravens

thin moon

and the snow
just whirrs

above the reef

                    *

I'm standing
in water

scales rising

I'm standing
in sleep

far bird

silver flows
bright scales

I'm standing

above
below

*

Wave
over wave

shell spirals

wave
over wave

whale turns

I'm dreaming
fishwings

inside me
I'm dreaming

old moon
bone moon

As the voice
lifts

a goose calls
farther

above the shattered crests
of this world

a dark head
rears the sky's

pale antler
hoists

what light remains
snared

in earthen throats

III.

OTHER LIGHTS

My desire is for the lightning and its gleam
—Ibn Arabi

LEGENDS

Other lights three
brilliant spheres
and us mute
stones
upon the ground

*

Now about the violet
whose sorrow darkened
until it reached
her heart so
bright

*

Or the one set
as a song a rumble
as the mountain
suddenly rose
to spin on a fingertip

*

Story of a sailor
whose luck quickened
when he awoke
married to the daughter
of salt and seaweed

*

Tell yet another
how colors came about
how a poor man prospered
how coal turned to diamond
how the sun rose once more how

*

All these tales
are really forests
where the woodcutter
and his wife raise
a child in secret

Openings

Out to open
this

space like a leaf

*

To be one with
purpose

a rod lightning-struck

*

Lost shards
offered up

earthfuls of light

*

This yearning after
yearning of a dark

to be laced with light

*

Breath on the dark
ladder with silver rungs

up and down and up

*

Silence split by this
voice

and made whole

Soft Lightnings

High chord
struck

the rose opening

sounds
in the heart

a bell

*

Freshness
within

uplifted

pure
the silver dish

brims

*

Space where
light springs

a fountain

taste clear
beyond water

beyond tongue

*

Far more than
this light

this stillness

clearest eye
or snow's promise

far more

*

Vibrant arc
that moon

radiates

from the center
we beam

in response

*

Discern that place
built of

soft lightnings

there within
the friend

dwells

THRESHOLD

Who waits
at the seams
of the apparent

while everything
nods in assent

    *

Always climbing
each step
a step

up to a step
to climb

    *

Image to hold
as a banner
the king dancing

on the threshold
of light

    *

Seems
an abyss but
a bridge

letting go
learning to move on

*

May the heart
know the way
to approach

that is the threshold's
threshold

*

Crossing over
one is carried
in its wake

a wind from beyond
opens all the doors

WINGS AND SUN

Turning
the lock
with a feather

my hope
rises like
a line of birds

*

Open wide
the ear the sound
of wings

lifting
the beyond
beyond

*

Climb
the bright
arc of its going

call reaching
the very
place of light

*

Chevron
aglint
at the zenith

straight up
the searing delegate
of height

*

Weave
a nest of sun
of moonlight

may that
bird alight
once more

*

Above
the blue
quivering world

wings and sun
twin emblems
of the word

Dome

Word as the echo
of a heartbeat

resounding in a house
with an ivory dome

       *

Dome of light
crowning the heart

opens its
secret halls

       *

Air rich with one
sound one stillness

song rising beneath
the dome of the unborn

       *

Tracing the circumference
of the journey

iridescent
the velocity of the turn

*

Glimpsed the script
etched round the apex

lines opening
a window beyond

*

In that brilliance
the uncertain becomes apparent

tongue and silence
wed to that dawn

Eostre

And risen is this
even above
death

aloft and yet
not lonely

*

Though one
light
fans into rays

bent to be
white again

*

*I can come to life
even under
the stone*

speechless
this witness listens

*

Speak plainly
a star in each heart
shines

not only in words
but lights

*

Simple this dawnlight
a being an angel
Eostre

natural as all
these risings

*

To end with A
is to start again
alpha aleph alif

more than mere faith
in new beginnings

Note: *Eostre, Anglo-Saxon goddess of dawn.*

Questing

for Lakshmi and Muhasibi

An inexpressible call
has come

not from within
nor without

not from the right
nor left

not from above
nor from below

you may ask
what direction is that

that direction
where there is questing

Jelal-al-Din Rumi

1

Beyond this space
of perforated darks

a field of light
opens up

carrying us as far
as a body can go

there begins
a new life

* * *

This yearning to move
across the earth

like an arrow that urges
the bow to bend

toward release

toward that quickened
silence

a poem can achieve
when lips form

the word *goal*

* * *

We give ourselves
over entirely

to the beyond

the attraction
that binds the elements

pulls us home

* * *

Silence the seed
the unspoken
must

to unfold
break the confines
let the husk fall

to be all opening
seeking
the brilliant one

glowing seed
turn us green
with light

* * *

The quest is a gesture
toward
what persists

tracing a figure of light

a reaching out
in itself
an offering

a thrust that draws us on

* * *

And the heart moves

ahead
to the place it knows

has built
out of patience

our longing cuts the door

2

Out of the place of shadows

and the ash whitening
down

still a flame can be seen

here
and in the sky and

beyond

    * * *

Itinerary of the quest

there is a place
you can reach
by going nowhere

voice of the old one
echoing
as we go on

and then memory
unwinding
tales of encounters

in the deep woods
a lamp always
flickering

just ahead

* * *

But suddenly
the sense of being
caught

in a thicket

trying to remember
the silver thread
still connects

up and out

as the thorns
scratch
their message

still deeper

though the dark
looks darker
look into the dark

and say *light*

* * *

Stone on stone
beneath the sign
of the wanderer

so one goes down
the road called
'no road'

* * *

These modes of perseverance
form the lessons of the quest

like a trial of moss
against stone

ordeal of the twig
tossed into the fire

or the root still
alive underground

                * * *

Seeking the grotto of voices
or the still place
at the center
of the rose

here even
stone is perfected
renders its presence
so close

and the scent
pervades space a fragrance
that leads
beyond fragrance

as if
in the distance
a hum rises
on the other side of sound

3

Tines of light
in the distance
brilliant

leading us
over the tundra
of the page

down
the sudden cleft
into another country

where the world
comes alive
again

for us
as we touch
our heads to the ground

and whisper
in curls of breath
these lines

* * *

Necessity of praise
as the wind

behind us

opens the road
and the heart

to whatever
light may be

breaking

above the peak
farther on

* * *

To make a way
to the farthest
point

wake
in a new land
of unnamed fruits

and see
beyond the fresh
colors

the untrod paths
that scale
the horizon's oneness

whiteness

* * *

Come back
to the ancient
dream at last

lay your head
on the seeing
stone and return

climb with
the bright ones
the central stair

you must touch
that high oil
to earth

* * *

By the door
to the forest
beckoning

a guide
with a map
of light

* * *

In the arcing birds
the twirling leaves

I read only
messages of going

see the new road
etched within

without

4

True orient

the heart bends
toward

climb
that steep rise

within

    * * *

Were we caught up

or did it touch
down

that no place
that fills

did it open out
a sudden

flower
in the straw

or enclose us
forever

the deepest bud

    * * *

Going and coming
are the legs
that carry us

we who
have become
entirely *approach*

silent as the stars
arrange themselves
above the gate

the combination
that springs open
the way home

* * *

The wound is a path
if torn by an eagle

pain and a way
beyond pain

you may find that
scar to be a map

leading to the place
where you belong

* * *

Hunting the call
to union

the swan keeps
circling the shore

* * *

Las voces que soplaron en el aire
formaron en el aire una ciudad
—Homero Aridjis

Out of ourselves
was built

crystal by crystal

an inestimable
place

massive yet minute

in a space above
space

the city

and our breath
the irradiant road

IV.

PINNACLES AND OTHERS

At Pinnacles

PINNACLES

> *Le lieu et la parole sont d'une même constellation.*
> —Jean Laude

HIGH PEAKS VIA CONDOR GULCH

Undulant rock forms
here

arisen
a terrestrial surging

thrust on thrust

and coming out
into the sun

just red-green
stone

then golden

in that light
going down

*

Voice like
a lizard quick

among mute stones

adjectival and hot
ready to flee

into some crevice
or seam

some fissure in speech

     *

What is this
red branch a magenta
rising

to say itself out
in green at last
manzanita

here
among stones and stone
forces

a flower

     *

And so the human goes
a walker

with a stick once
a twig
on some high tree

north of here
bent by the wind now
bending over meaning

of flower
of stone
of dust

     *

Pitch ecstatic
above the pinnacles
chi-a
chi

the songbird's
birdsong

source unseen

                *

Slow rodeo of condors
absent

this noontime

only one lone
hovering

wing on the updraft
circumambulant

above Chalone

high peak
with its fringe of ruins

                *

The old chief's song –

above my head
you will hear
the hummingbird
when this world
comes alive again

and you will see
him too – flashing
then lighting
here – now
do you?

*

Ancient volcano
eroding home

*

Chalk then
ash perhaps the spent

fire of a cone
gone solid

tossed back
transmuted

into the air
a geology triumphant

through the twisted
agency of a branch

*

I go seeking a nectar
cooled in the center
of each flower

sprung from powdered
magma risen once
from the core

and who is ancestor
to both stone and flower

but the sun

flower
imaged in the form
of sol and I
the solaced one

it is the sun's honey
I drink

and through seeing
thump the heart

*

Hawk
in the high air

below me
seeking constantly

over your shadow
a sign that flickers

among dry grasses
cracked sticks packed

earth
an arroyo seco

*

Chaparral of waking
and dreaming waking

*

Among and into
the whistles of birds

lost
the voice moves on

over the shattered path
the chaparral of the lipless

I lean into the solitude
of those whistles

       *

Composition of air
tapped out
on strings of moving things

the alto wind articulates
the sparse measure
of trees

(these letters take the shape
of leaves)

       *

Quiet
the voice of the toyon

atop the pinnacles
singular among the crows'

caw-haw
haw-caw

a cadence all quivers

       *

Ancient rockslide
now all violet

wildflowers with golden
tips folded like birds
dark beaks to the stem
'shooting stars'
flickering in the windy
sundown brilliance
transparent

      *

(Moses' Spring)

here the last cave
you can discern water
tapping its poem
out in a trickle
from the mountain's center

syllables of sky
said through stone

ALONG THE BALCONIES

Under oak at last a place
to quiet down
corral the breath
recount the climb
loop by loop
to trace the path
through pine stand
stone field
to arrive at last
at the great peace
as the pulse
settles down

*

Far cave
perfect circle

an ear in stone
of the earth

a channel
to the earth listening

to the squawking
archaeopteryx or crow

cave where each
particle chip bit

every sedimentary fleck
presents its own

presence unique each
lime-orange lichen

painting the wall
as if the brush of Seurat

was taken
each morning

      *

Give voice to the lichen cuneiform
across serpentine rock
same as seen atop
Twin Peaks but here
laced over with green
and orange and this non-color
alluding to a gray
grown over stone
as we utter syllables
urged into words
outcroppings heaved
up and adorned
with this filigree
of knowing not
knowing

      *

Slice of cliff face
a stranded moon
below in the chaparral
I
can only question echoes
why shamans left
these walls so blank
seems they held this
unadorned upthrust
too sacred to touch

even with spirit yet
moss flares into form
five distinct figures
step forward
haloed in a golden
green light
like painted flames
in a paler glow
it too greenish
this beyond

                *

Though infinite
depth is not
possible a chasm
space between
upright stones
may be a frame
a door for beings
visaged in stone
beyond and imaged
out of it

                *

To set off a yantra
for buddhas to appear
in this American canyon
where plates grind
across eons
tectonic spirits
around which tiny birds
fly nameless from here
but whistle still
the high note
mantra of stone
under sky

                *

Flight and the poem
set vertigo in motion
as I trip
toward the yet to be
spanned abyss

(bridge of fragile speech)

only the body halts
the skid
gravel rains

stones plummet

*

(prayer)

Red spirit forms
emergent

from lime-green
nimbi here

give me spring
poems

*

But a token should be left
a talisman
carried inside
so I leave you red pebble
tiny heart as an offering
an homage
to the abiding presence
just as Mongols
set stones in piles
obos

in holy places or dire
to acknowledge the presiding
spirit seek protection
or guidance
along the narrowing path
or simply
to stay alive

*

Lemon stone over
the oak

a grounded moon
ear hoisted
above a rare basin
of still water

La Nuestra de Señora de Soledad
Mirror of Our Lady
(Alone)

*

Wee poem of adios
beneath oak and juniper boughs

North Wilderness

First to the windy mission
before the climb
to strike the ancient
bell once more
Ave Maria Purisma
Anno Domini
1799

and then
beneath the eaves
sheltering birdsong
and blown roses
counting aloud the twenty-three
vigas exposed overhead
to emerge in the end
among golden poppies to find
the early graves of two Spaniards
one governor Arrilaga
one priest Ibañez
both Franciscans
soldier or shepherd
gone to the ground
here alone

Soledad

＊

Into the chaparral
taking the unknown path
by the white creekbed
past lifeless oaks
detailed in Spanish moss

I seek out fresh growth
amid gnarled gray some nodes
like sparks the vegetal
fire kindled in dark
shining delight

                  *

Beyond the tossed
stone piled on twisted stone
into bee fields of saxifrage
wild pansy or something golden faced
defining its reflection
by another in another
rooted beyond a common description
each opens a voice
if only a vowel
that moves through
a mouth of wind

                  *

Angel of the pathway
lifting pentafoil wings
seeking its friend
through the agency of the bee
may these words
be as bees
come from solitary hives
the silent
flight the search for a sweetness
that tastes of the sun

                  *

Little lizard beneath the pine
come to me
here by the greatest thistle
ever to rise
whose red solar tip is just dawning

hey he leaps onto the bark
twirls around the bole
blends into the world

go back to your house
near the village of crickets

buenas noches my friend
Don Lagarto
don't worry
I won't eat you

       *

At Pinnacles
you can penetrate
beyond the apparent
see into what builds
behind a landscape
as if for a moment the hidden
manifests in a finger of stone
a dome of wildflowers
even a rough sage bush
a dry canyon oak

       *

Leaning into the striated
blue the last
upthrusts of magmatic stuff
old stone poems
unworded 23 million
an ago unuttered before
these efforts
unerected monuments
to solitude

Garrapata
  for Perrin

> *Come eyes, see more than you see!*
> *for the world within and the outer world*
> *rejoice as one....*
> —Robert Duncan

You must go down the canyon
past the callas and briars
the cactused slope
to where the voice can start again
regain its ring *en printemps*
even the dry hills
give water here Rancho
San Jose y Sur Chiquito
along the south coast
a place called Garrapata

    *

Home searcher
goes it alone

up over lichened rock
among the furled poppies
each a banner of the golden horde

and these violet ones
wonders growing inward
and outward all around

the bees of spring

                    *

Silver trunk moss-chewn
toppled now a bridge
over the twirling creek
its offspring sempervirens
rise red-barked

I will go deep
into this redwood stand
stilled by its stillness
yet drawn to form
words out of a ring
of silence

                    *

Ancient thought
slow to emerge
but pure
        o
deep one

Being-in-the-Form-of-Redwood

may my voice
be your voice
your stillness
open my mouth

I place my hand
on the bark the vital
power of this

site specific
and sacred to the one
energy

*

Poem on the stone
path of heaven
up the far side of Palo Corona
by a crevasse long dry
I one
atop the wind
above the redwood canyon

noting my own high
presence here
in the presence of these hills

no reason to doubt it
coil of the city
unsprung
by evident commonality

*mountain stone
flower hu-
man*

rainbow around the sun
a sea-mist
over the high peak
breaks into prismic light

cattle off
in the distance
low in what fold
what canyon

perhaps it is only
the echo of dragonfly
or the whir
through the stillness

some far bee

*

All over this mountain

I too am now
a bee of seeking

all over this mountain

a thistle profound
with latent
honey

*

Why am I not a painter
a devotee of purest color

verdigris moss on purple stone
this yellow rock amid whitening sage
a turquoise shirt before
a green triangle against
the clearest blue

I too portrayer of gray
brush the blackened
sticks dried by a thousand noons

and here a twirl of brightness
alyssum
rousing the hive

drink the drink of light
with the eye
of the god

    for Johnny Apodaca

*

Around the shoulder of a hill
Sol my star

through the eye
ajar enter
most clear light

flood the roads
in my heart

*

Again I will seek
the water's source
in woods
where all paths diminish
to one of water
where the deer nuzzle
the green air
about the moss-drenched rock

*

Pang in the Bodhisattva
gesture

mudra
of the open flower

this healing through
nature
native to each

caritas immanentis San Fran-

cesco might have thought
once

an awe
mends the wound
hopes the heart
to go on

we need to be
tied in
by hand by voice
by art
to follow that yearning

to replicate
the soul-need always
to form or be
born

I would put my tongue
in the service
of the one
effort

as the bee does
its buzz

*

Marvelous to stand
by the root of a tree
the stream penetrates
dives beneath

to emerge away
among three sequoia

leaning into the last
sunbeams

      *

Señor frog
may I hear your poem

silence
a frightened frog
(my stressed heart)

only water sounds
compose the poem
of water

hee-beep
hee-beep
beep-hee-beep

we both await the moon

      *

Moon like a magenta
thistle lofts
atop the redwood towers
looms above Soberanes Creek
pales to a pacific

o

      *

(Ridgeway)

no sound but the wind
and a bird
on the wind a whistle
to my cupped ear
held like Milarepa

all awed by the rush
of air
open-jawed
for the poem of it

Garrapata

Note: *Garrapata* – Garrapata Canyon and environs, along the Big Sur
coast.

Reciting Signs

You are a sign and the seeker
after a sign
what better sign than the seeker
after a sign
Jelal-al Din Rumi

All I ask is permission
To stand here waiting
And that you will give me a sign
From within myself of yourself!
Gunnar Ekelöf

Whether at loss
or in finding

tell me the shape
of that light
which opens

space
a wound or world

door
through each cell
to the other

tell me what is
the shape of that
pain

this seeking
a form for the formless

face without a face

*

If in this venture
toward union
we all make

that you and I might
be privileged
to find in each

an aperture on
the roomful of light
and so make actual

that Amida land
in blended glance
or hand quivering

we are dual paradises
melding up as well
as down

in this space
demarked by cups of Kenya
AA

*

That I have become this
bell
resonant to your tone
your presence

who is to blame

my sudden appearance
on the threshold
as if awaiting your call

or your calling

should my patience
be augmented
by invisibility

my word turbaned
in inaudibility

trepidation is a bat
turning among lightning
flashes

what remains
only the prayer
of the rocking devotee

*leave me this
insight
but let me assimilate it*

*

Then there is this silence
at the verge of your lip
where I turn iridescent
as the night fills with
your word
my room is luminous
until I wake
to find myself
out on the patio
at Caffe Cardinale
facing the palest rose
color of your eyelids
whose scent recalls
the inner taste
ecstatic still

of the place where
we met first

*

I will gather
these distances
into a bouquet of roads

there is a silvery bird
who will not sing
whose presence
turns my sky vivid
and blue

this muteness
attracts the inverted
pyramid of yearning
whose peak touches down
on this heart

even Carmel has a hundred
miles of road

*

Should I inscribe
an anchor
upon my finger
sign of the constant
and the state I was born in
whose motto rises
an opal moon
on the tongue
'hope'
let me stay in the dark
in the outer circle
with that word
as my lamp

my mantra
until your heart lights
my heart my
bright one

       *

      My poore hert bicomen is hermyte
      In hermytage of thoughtfulle fantase
           —Charles of Orleans

When you do not call
I become the secluded
anchorite of Garrapata

my door shuts
solitude upon solitude
when you do not call

certitude seems conjecture
my prescience a phantasm
our consonances dismissed

still I know this is real
a *fin'amor* here and now
but when you do not call

I am bereft of bells
the mellifluous promptings
of your questions

my message machine spins
and spins
when you do not call

I go farther up the mountain
to listen with an ear
beyond hearing

as the hermit sharpens
with waiting his spirit
against the wind

                *

This much is known

'my soul
the first time I saw you
my soul heard something
from your soul'

did Mevlana see
you with my eye
in Konya then

did he inscribe
with the pen
of your visage

your presence
on the tabula rasa
of my unborn soul

you are to be found
among the vowels
that interlace
these lines that resonate

this much is known

                *

Out in the rain

filling at last
the antique basin
with its filigree of tendrils

I stand among the pavers
talking to the sky

a gesture of breath
toward an ancient notion

something about your radiance
and a sensation of wings
in the chest

so I will rename this courtyard
in the Directory of Inwardness

Place des exiles de la lumière

then place another
votive
in the empty niche

      *

Once quite early
I heard your voice
pronounce my name
a farewell or greeting
distinct and within
then again toward eleven
something so clear
came through
my heart suddenly opened
are these bodies really
essential
privileges or encumbrances
these places necessary
this California
a requisite
for the high
desire that lifts
and bears us

Point Pinos

Point Pinos
a. b. c. proposed Sites
X. Y. lines exhibiting the range of visibility of
proposed light.
Scale 1/20,000
Y

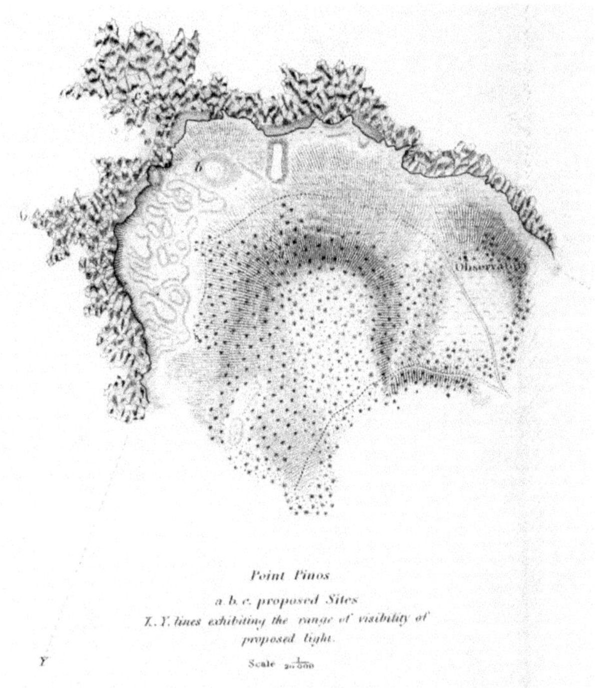

Point Pinos

This time I will follow
the angel
through speckled woods
'the house of wings'
to listen
the distinct waves
sound as one
fog encircles Monterey
pines the woodpecker
types his own story
light breaks through
a hidden bee hums
the moment
I join in
with poem the distant
chimes through
all of it

*

Eucalyptus grove
I stride by
as prayerflags
loosen their letters
the sun at this declination
fills the eye lights
the nervous system

I am drawn by the apparent
tipping of a star
toward the horizon an ocean
so pacific
children sing by the tidepool
nine pelicans cross the sun
I gaze over the water
path of flickering
luminosity
om ah hum
one might mantra

     *

Beyond the vacant
frontage of the affluent
where seascent and salt
mix with pungent sage
I stumble crabwise
along the deckled
edge of Asilomar
overnight the tide
uprooted stands of kelp
tentacles hurled and knotted
a rotting brim to this cove
driven off by the human
below the scan of raucous gulls
I yearn to go
in search of quiet pools
where the small things
make love

     *

Mariposatree
transparent

at sun's tilt
a million wings
I am en-
tranced by the motions
of the nonhumans
and sense new wings
we are a-dance
before the only
monarch Sol
astir

*

I skirt the coast
lean into the west
for glint on spout
of sundown whale
then glimpse
the lamp whose beam
seeks the horizon
signs
the name of evening
'Point Pinos'
since the Yankees came
your simple cut
your flash
pledges hope

*

Woods loft into
the blue
purpling to dusk
last beams know me
well
I seek

solace in the west
among pines
on the peninsula's end
birds lift
their hosannas
impervious to this
soul's drone into
the wind

*

Gray water hauled
back to the horizon
without whale
or sound
even the trawler stalls
miles off
a sudden miniature wave
one then another
always from the south
comes a pelican
skimming the mirror
you can sense
the Santa Cruz
rim of the bay
below the blue
gray a remoter
blue or shimmer

*

Birds cross overhead
in the shape of a bird
so the world makes metaphor
my role is simple
jotting it down

no kenning after
meaning of 'skyroad'
the vates are gone now
who could count such
swift birds
meter the variant
spins in the moment
that wobble the future
with wish

Pacific Grove, California

V.

NIGHTSCRIPTS

When I arose and saw the dawn
I sighed for thee

—Shelley, "Ode to the Night"

NIGHTSCRIPTS

To open perhaps
a journal of days
or nights
looping their silences
over the months
as the white light
levels and opens perhaps
even all of it

*

Script of this
air
this starlight
the twittering crickets
out writing
the book of September
all night
behind the boxes
one lone one
this small voice
chiming in

*

These first efforts
the voice breaking
its chains
one by one
making its noise
if not joyful maybe
quavering
waking its way
home

*

The dream itself
locked
on the outside

    *

You can go on
about utterance
its ability to rinse
you in light
break even the tiniest
links that silence
the heart

    *

Dulled by
the ebb of wakefulness
sleep dusting down
a mist
leaving us drenched
with yawning
still yearning

    *

So night grows
on to a day
vanquished in details
until another
darkness opens
its soft blankness
filtering starlight
making it possible
all of it

Page Toward a Book of Beginnings

Silence
eclipsing itself in a whir

a song goes out
in search of a throat

breaking into
light into

circles of opening
a dilation of worlds

sings up an ocean
winged song finned song

sings a man a woman
the slow hum of mountains

and the briefest
of canticles

day flickering
on a leaf

A Field of Shadows

I am black and beautiful
        — Solomon's Song

My dark opens out
to your light

     *

Black one
nighting my day

     *

Crowswoops
from a former tree

     *

Trail of my heels
moving on with me

     *

A darkness fetched
up to the moon

     *

Shade of the rose
she sleeps in

     *

I dream in your dark
of my light

Astroglyphs

Moonless
the sky thick
with hope

clear gaze
opening space
a light-hour

*

Ancient light
your thin beam
splits a prism

you bend over
a billion
years

*

Another galaxy
recedes
beyond sight

another eyelid
shut on
remoteness

*

Pure distance
this thrust
in all dimensions

traceless
the void stares
without a face

   *

Just space
a nothing squared
by nothing

the lack of
say
a hunk of iron

   *

So earth too
is
a beyondness

from any point
out there
infinity rays

   *

Transpierced
all emptiness
pulsates

the night
gone white
overhead

CALL

Into the bright
and endless whirl

beyond stillness

a snow filling
the night and every
step on the path

in the heart
there is no darkness

only an albino deer
who among
the whitening pines

sniffs and bells

The Blue Hour

Awaiting
the night's condensation

a song of going

light beading
on the brim of the sky

a story told

holding aloft a glass
once more

a dream returning

to catch a taste
of starlight

TABLE OF KHAYYAM
for Pir Vilayat

Somewhere
outside the precincts
they are lifting
tiny glasses
with fingers of light
their rings made of light
gleaming as they clink
and to the lips
'dawn over the ocean'
that rosy beverage
taste without senses
brilliant eyes everyone
laughing about nothing
and everything

A Child

Our own arises
this year

a star holy with
newness
in the womb's

deep sky

a hope we can
grow with
too

the three of us
conjoined
enjoining oneness

this first of the year

Perrin on his way

THE HIDDEN

Stone in the heart
let the angel
come

open the chest
with one

touch of a wing

and raise you
lapis

luminous

to shine
room upon room

Forecast

So the light
moves
toward a fulfillment

some distant 'west'

and our small lives
work themselves
increment by increment

toward a taste of it

even the slightest
like the scent
of seafoam tossed

into the air

sensed inland
one hundred miles

FIVE WINTER PROSE POEMS

Early Snow

Holding a dim beam and walking into a night bent with snow
and starlight. This track cuts across a whiteness looking for
a way down to the river. Never to be lost again – though the
snows return and the world grows dim with sudden blankness.
The night will be before you even if you cannot light the lamp.

Around the Solstice

You watch the sky for a measurable sign. Who could discern
the lengthening of light? Somewhere there's a gyro, an atomic
clock. You dream of birds arriving in waves but their perches
are distant – a blue green continent southerning away. The cat
curls tighter. My temperature climbs another notch. The town
is cut off by a hard rain mixed with snow. You might call this a
charm for returning.

Too Much January

Iced into dry rooms. The barometer dwindles. Rust spreads un-
der fenders, blossoms from hidden places. My joints flare then
it snows. Chains clink and the road salt clicks all night. Come
morning your window will be pale. Baseball gods still under-
ground. Too much January.

Headcold

Thieves seal you into the cavern of treasures – a lamp flutters. A closed nostril jolts you out of the dream of peace. By the window the mercury settles below zero but beneath my tongue tops one double zero. Wrapped in chills Acetaminophen marches into the Gobi of headache. When your nose is gone the entire face becomes a lip. Let this small prayer go in lieu of a curse: may this be the last if the worst of the season.

Last Snow

Almost May the wet snow brought down a limb from the dogwood – a white plume in the vanishing whiteness. Long grasses doubled over, pale leafings and purple flowers, the verdigris-tinged boughs wet-dark… A lone contemplator ties it together – knitting needles silent to a robin's call. My boy trudges ahead puddle by puddle, throws his hat in the snow, runs in red boots toward summer.

Providence, Rhode Island

TURNING ROUND
for E.

To begin again see
the wave of good happening
break overhead
and look
that uniform slab of cloud
suddenly opens to the blue
and somehow always there
promise just for you
a providence if you will
a real one

Aftershocks

(after Ibn Arabi)

I

Their houses are crumbling
yet my desire to live here
remains unabated

I weep over toppled stairways
still my heart melts when I recall
their beauty

allured I lusted after Jaguars
shouting - *you who are so rich
look at me a beggar*

homeless I humbled myself
in the dust
do not leave me hopeless

seared by the flame of despair
I nearly drowned in my own tears
yet no one came to help

look you who would like to start
another fire
you need but stir theses embers

II

Desire seeks the uplands
sadness the lowlands

so I'm lost between
San Francisco and Los Angeles

these opposites cannot be joined
my shattering ever be put together

how should I be - what should I do
guide me please don't blame me now

sighs rise like prayers
tears raining down

my aged MG gasps on the grade
whines like a crazed lover

when the gasket goes at last
I will be primed for annihilation

good-bye my life good-bye
my patience

San Francisco-Monterey

AN AIR FOR THE DEPARTED

on my parents' passing

That silence circles
these moments

an array of muted nows

remains the quivering
truth

amid the pummeling
hours

the instants
bow the blossoms
like rain

it is grief's requirement
to intone
a simple phrase

ask even your own
echo so basso
profundo

they go do they why do they
go

perhaps there is a way
to follow

lift a single word
a wing
that frees you as you
circle

circle now

ORB MUSIC

And it expands in circular form...this realm
secure and full of gladsomeness, full of
ancient people and modern....
                    —Dante, *Paradiso*

They have the next
life
up here

men women
their gone beauty
delicate alive
still

there is a true place
like not like
a sky or void

no bitter death
but an urge to leave
time behind

for an enormous power
like the sun

Early in Fez

Flight from the continent's edge
toward the world's center
to Fez

labyrinth of hope
that might lead at last
beyond myself

to wake in the dark
medina
coiled like the cochlea

and listen
for a tracery of sound

arabesque
cadence of distant
footfalls low voices

gates shut or opened

discern at the extent
of hearing

the muezzin's call
amid the dawn's first
birding

GODDESS POEMS

Give us Astapis,
Let Philylla look this way,
       Damareta and lovely Wianthemis.
For Hagesikhora we long.

     —Hymn to Artemis… Alkman (7 c. BCE)

PHOENIX CALL
   for BeBe

A silent call
struck
me to resonate

gong in that
dark where souls
resound

so I came
down the Coast Highway
to Nepenthe
'land of no sorrow'
 the Phoenix place

and you

by the stair
peered with gray
eyes into my deep
space
to where a wing
rises free
from the heart's ash

and all the signs
say be just be

      * * *

Russian New Year
    for Svetlana Chaikina

Your voice breaks
fragile wave
on this shore
but goes unheard

even so
far inland
a tired wing lifts
a seagull cries
chai-kin-a-chai

above the vermilion
curve of the Dneiper
as it slows by rosebud domes

and no one remembers
that you are gone

it is so hard
to live in a place
where poetry is dismissed

here the native cadence
derives from the ledger
even poets mouth
songless prose

ahead you see
a golden city
it scintillates
in your palm
'all is light'

I could only offer
some moments to shelter
at the continent's edge
at year's end
in this poem

* * *

MESSAGE IN WINTER

Since what was
taken for limitation
was the vastness
I gave
so plunges another
glacier
into a birdless ocean
and vanishes beneath
what you might never know
to where a whale
turns and dives
to deep his moan

* * *

You came a particular wave
of light

your senses lengthening
toward the infinite

miming the word
'possible'

with every gesture
of eyes

but even as you gleamed
you veered away

from what might
have shone

had two flares
twined

say who was preserved
from union

by the mirror's flash
bright one

* * *

GODDESS

> *So bright is the light that shines from you*
> *I need balm for my eyes*
>
> anon, ancient Egypt
>
> *for Carolyne*

The heart opens
it is the point of song

the vertebrae click
vessels pulse
to the joy of it

this one who unkeys
wholeness

the goddess steps
forward proffering
a tone

in a cipher of sound
the encoded one
she

bears the plentitude
of light

Aubade

Hovering before us
the solar cup
of the lovers

we go seeking
the tryst
of both worlds

our desire is
a dawned-upon rose

DOVES

In the bush
one white-winged
chants plainly
(a flutter) another
her respondent
tops the utility
ascetic of light
ecstatic warbles 'I am
a symbol!' yes
not only descendant of dinos -
archaeopteryx – but
silvery hiero-
glyph of transcendent
hope a call
gone skyward

A Table at Florian's
   for Henry and Suzanne Lennard

When I think of you
I arrive in Venice
San Marco is tinted
rose-gold

I inhale and sense
a high purpose
with no purpose
as we lift café
in the vastness
of a cosmos which is
the piazza

before the musicales
we are talking again
about platonic ideas
someone declares the double
helix is the archetype
the pigeons rearrange themselves

it is clear
all the passersby
personae
masks of the only
we mug commedia dell'arte
faces and nod

friends I salute you
stone lions still
roar through our souls

MARTYR OF BAGHDAD

Dismembered city whose suffering
forms the image of the obliterated
mystic

Baghdad of lovers
whose domes still moan
the name of the beloved

Mansur

his blood every droplet
writes the great name
as it flows to the Tigris

name once again
the ash of that incense
that lover

Hallaj

whose love becomes oneness
as the word that forms all
forms in a mouth

an utterance
that reiterates through
every true lover

an'l haq

in a whisper
to the core of each
core

Note: *Mansur al-Hallaj, Sufi mystic poet (d.309 AH/913 CE); an'l haq
(I am the Truth).*

Cardona

in memory, Monserrat Figueras

205

Lofted to the high
perch of Cardona
by birdsong

the whir and swing
the swallow's dance
above towers lit
by rosy sundown

forget the dukes
befriending the quick
and the dead

let us wake between
the walls of singers
and saints

Vegetal

As the present always
evokes so
the root uncurls
a primal effort
to become entirely
green now
just as (even
the moment improving
itself) the wild-
flower
declares the purplest
urge to announce
a golden center
first bees yet
to be seen
the snows relinquish the treeline
birds all praise
the sun god
earthworms twirling
the compost to life

A Local Variant of Rimbaud's *Voyelles*

A (black) - E (white)
I (red) - O (green)
U (purple)
Vowels now I am
free to tell
my own creation myths

A - all
the flies in black
leather jackets buzzing
down the shadowy canyon
toward Los Alamos' megaton workshops
brisk business of assembling
an apocalypse
in potentia

E – eternal
white of Loretto's spires lifting
the mountain over Santa Fe
Lady of Light
an encampment of cloud
or village of bright
kachinas
rising above a mist
that settles down
on the snowy tips of grasses

I - innocent
blood the crimson
choked up
the mute victim

and then
the inquisitor's smirk
just rise above it
this penitente levitates

O - oceanic
waves viridian and calm
coextensive with divinity
peace of mammals
whose sacred syllables
are imprinted on the glowing
forehead of the environmentalist

U – unseen
sounds the horn
piercing the cells opens a door
shaped like an omega
for an angel to step through
violet flash of the eye
goddess
above an extinct ocean

Santa Fe, New Mexico

OURAY

Up to Ouray
where troubles dwindle
as the ice recedes
among the spidering paths
the self regains its green
along the melts
the streams that cross
crisscross these ways
amid rocks and snow
and trees

GRASSHOPPER

Inquiring of
a greenness greener than
Eire

I lean close but
render no fearsome
gesture

what if I were you
an ingenious
weed-dancer

leap now
wee sir
perch and peer

with an oblong
look
head cocked

antennae akimbo
sensing into the present
the only world

POET IN HIS ORCHARD
for James McGrath

He discards care
wears instead
a jaunty hat
as the wind picks up
he leans and smiles
into the vivifying feel of it
his own omnipresence
blown around among
apple-blossoms iris the nameless
up-popping small greens
he notes each one
speaks them if not into being
into a presence better yet
written than ephemeral
his is a vernal autumn
him second-sensing the mushroom
mycelia fanning out underground
his foot on this earth
let's celebrate
its spring and lilt its uplift
in the dance

Autumnal

Into a morning
waking
without expectation
but holding

a hope
speckled egg
in the nest
of the may yet
to come

I go on
without message
or text
awaiting no one

and release
the unmet omissions

minor or large
disregards dissolve
oblivion like

smoke
from the Sangres
into the horizon's
paling zone

WAY OF THE DEAD
(in the necropolis of Arles)

Sarcophagi line the path
rough conveyances
toward another life

a lost hagiography of parted lovers
writ over stele and slab
here a heart chiseled on a shield
a motto inscribed in imagined
late Latin...*could never be
better than ours...*

below the lantern tower
among the remnants
of a gone chapel
three distant figures
linger like Gauguin's
graces or guides
to Elysium
Alyscamps

I will wait by
the once gateway
an architecture for oblivion
roof gone
to point the way

I lift
a palm full of shadow
salute the inscrutable unknown

THE LAST VISIT
with Edwin Honig

What is becomes
was and so
it is a move-
ment a present into
a now
that's always
nowing

*just as light
shifts on leaves*

the poet gestures

I touch his arm
in a moment that
now was

PEERING THROUGH A CRACK
BETWIXT WORLDS THE ONCE
HIERONYMUS SURVEYS THE GOINGS ON

Firstly one
fish-faced pitches
the unfounded
he frets over the gelatinous
mood of a man-o-war
among whose tentacles
he sways

            x

Medusa
of alternate facts
squirms in the direction of the drain
question is why
do this again
and again

            x

Disheveled but
debonair supreme
promulgator of the preposterous
there goes a sideways
mouth twisting
toward Armageddon

            x

That brassy boaster
blares at the bass
he'd blow his
own to disown
that horny strumpet

       x

Her chainsaw eye
carves an enormous eagle
and sticks it
in the front yard

       x

All the urinals are filled
with croc-headed representatives
the trouble is the stench
fills the entire house

       x

The titillated man with little
hands lifts
her cadillacs
celebrity's privilege
they just let you do it

       x

So the inhabitants sink
along with the island
while the very
very stable
with a good brain too
tosses bounties then thumps
on his twit stick

WAYS OUT OF WINTER

Palpable
out of serial
frozen days
I can just forecast
the budding branch
a smudge of ash
as the viral swirls
the first greens then
the news
a friend departs

*

I face the east
nuzzle the air
sniff for a change
(or eternal return)
just a hominid
leaning into extinction

*

Can I kindle
a small green flame
keep it going
despite panic or pandemic
winter's raucous end
the iris persists

*

Pronounce
the true name of a sudden
flower sprung
out of arid nowhere
emergent an ever
urge to manifest
even here
a force like healing
latent or inferred
whose only evidence
is itself

*

Walls up everywhere
here comes
the caravan of the hopeless
some out of personal
hells some collective
still clinging to the idea of spring

*

Wash your hands
the republic lurches into tyranny
Don't touch your face
folly grabs the orange crown

*

Perplexed
another day to measure
winter's damage
go to the calendar
museum closed
concert cancelled
limit groups to two
no longer a suggestion

another anonymous
whomever goes

*

Let's lift a wing
call in the beneficents
make up green medicine
pour a cup then
another this
for the absent other

Vernal Equinox 2020

On a Fragment by Novalis

Could light be but
a sign of the new union -
the visible
Genius of union
together?

*

Allure of the luminous
drawing us in
like bees

only to find a deeper
urge to inhere
meld a present

so make visible
the seamless cohesion
new union indeed

to be seen to see
deep through the lens
of the trilobite eye

deepest to the 14 billion
light-year wall
arc of all from then to now

photons beaming
from the quasar's ancient
early heart

Somnambulant Ballad

Without candle or word
another equinox passes
corners ink deeper
a lone voice moans
200,000 gone more a-goin'

as we sleepwalk toward November

in a small room in another place
lit only by a screen
a puppet show we're all in
shadow hands on the wall

as we sleepwalk toward November

from a perch atop the eagle
the boaster shouts out hoaxes
schemes aloud to slam
the future door

as we sleepwalk toward November

say her name *Breonna*
over and over *Breonna*
in our sleep *Breonna* sorry
we live a waking nightmare

as we sleepwalk toward November

sierras of flame animal cries
smoke domes over

the choking town
enough
close the window
turn inside

as we sleepwalk toward November

George Washington
appears at the back door
his known-to-all visage
plainly dismayed
omen like a moon

as we sleepwalk toward November

someone once asked
why can't we all
just get along despite
up steps and stumbles
with efforts redoubled

as we sleepwalk toward November

restless sleep
a sudden twinge startles
we shudder awake
e pluribus unum
on burning tongues

10/20

Migrant Words

Where is wherever
we can go

over the border
beyond
the land of Nod
safe at last

can we move on
under manna-filled clouds
and clap for joy
chant

incant *libertad*
motto of the deep heart's core

let's go engender yet
another life
to build a song in

Zero Hour

Now for a parenthesis
a glottal stop
hold the breath a beat

an *em* between letters
hiatus ample
enough to rest

like a stanza break
recumbent
verb outstretched

now poised to leap
cat-like between
then and next

To the Future Poets

Go speak the singular
lingo of wholeness

craft an image a new
uroboros to encompass
the all in all

despite the fact
of that and this
her or him
east west

be a voice for once
of oneness

Coda

The poet declares
you are one
with the elements

lived lives of water
lives of air
even as a fiery spirit

spent eons in the earth
a ruby among minerals

you dove you slithered
sang as you flew

spent eras as a mammal
grazing among mammals

now that you stand
upright and enclose
a human soul

turn toward the only
return to the one
the only

Song More Song More Song More Song More

Bird conjuring

NOTES

Cover
Adam Fuss: unique Ciba Chrome photogram from the series
"In Between." Born in 1961, Fuss was raised in Britain,
presently lives and works in New York City. Many exhibits,
monographs. Subject of an insightful essay by Eugenia Parry.

Bird Conjuring (half title page)
Epigraph from Roberto Juarroz' *Vertical Poetry*, 1988. W.S.
Merwin, translator.

'There is a Light...'
Title is from "De Profundis" by Georg Trakl, *Selected Poems,*
1968.
Michael Hamburger, translator.

Broken Water Frozen Light
Italics are words by Paul Celan (1920–1970), German-Jewish
poet, from *Speech-Grille and Selected Poems*, 1971. Joachim
Neugroschel, translator.

Aureole
In the painting by Geergen tot Sint Jans (Neth. 15 c.) the
Madonna and Child are surrounded by musical angels who
form an aureole or halo. The Infant chimes in, too, with a small
bell.

Moon of Blinding Snow
Third month of the Oglala (Sioux) year. Wounded Knee
Massacre occurred in 1890; protest and occupation, March
1973.

Raven's Boast
Raven: creator/trickster of Northwest Coast Indian myth.

Ghost Call
Section II: Kichtan and Hobbamocko are the two most powerful of the thirty-seven Manitou (spirit-beings) of the Algonquin tribes of southeastern New England. Kichtan is the Creator. He fashioned the other manitowock and carved the first people out of wood. Later, he sent them beans and corn through the intermediary of the crow. Dwelling far away in Sowwaniu (the spirit world in the southwest) he takes little interest in the affairs of human beings. On the other hand, Hobbamocko is directly involved with the forces of this world. Wampanoag and Narragansett shamans often entreated him. (See Roger Williams' *A Key into the Language of America, 1643.)*
Section III: Quotes describing the Norse sorceress are from "Eirik's Saga" (M. Magnusson and H. Palsson, translators), one of the two Icelandic accounts of the exploration of North America. (See *The Vinland Sagas,* 1965).
Woman who fills the sky is a phrase from Federico Garcia Lorca's poem "Your Childhood in Menton" (Edwin Honig, translator).
Section IV: 'lone block of stone' indicates the traditional death place of "King Philip" Metacom(et), Massasoit's son, sachem of the Wampanoag Indians and leader of the King Phillip's War (1676–1677) against settler encroachments.

Other Lights
Epigraph from *The Tarjuman al-Ishwaq* (Interpreter of Desires) by Ibn Arabi, R.A. Nicholson, translator. 1911.

Eostre
Anglo-Saxon goddess from whose name Easter was derived.

Questing
Epigraph paraphrased from Jelal al-Din Rumi, *Mystical Poems of Rumi,* 1968.
A.J. Arberry, translator.
"Going and coming" from "*Approach,*" a hexagram of the *I Ching.*

Pinnacles
Pinnacles is a formation and national monument located
astride the San Andreas fault east of Soledad, California.
Remnant of a once mile high volcano, Pinnacles has ridden
the Pacific plate over the past twenty-three million years to its
present location 195 miles northwest of its origin.
Photo, "At Pinnacles" by Perrin Cloutier.
Epigraph from Jean Laude *Le mur bleu,* 1964.
Chalone – high peak of the Pinnacles.
"The old chief's song" contains a fragment of my version of a
Tsimshian Indian song, collected by Marius Barbeau. The third
piece from the end translates and paraphrases a few lines from
"El Largado viejo" by Federico Garcia Lorca.

Garrapata
("tick"in Spanish). A creek and canyon between Carmel and
Big Sur, California.
Epigraph from Robert Duncan, "Variations on Two Dicta by
William Blake," from *Roots and Branches,* 1964.
Milarepa: Tibetan poet-yogi often depicted cupping his ear to
hear the unheard sound.

Reciting Signs
Amida (Amithaba) – Buddha of the Western Paradise.
fin'amor (Provencal): true or real love, the troubadour ideal,
often unrequited, as evidenced by spiritual ardor, tests and
longing.
Mevlana - "Our Master", honorific title of Jelal al-Din Rumi,
Persian poet and mystic.
Epigraph is from Gunnar Ekelöf, *Selected Poems,* 1971. W.H.
Auden and Leif Sjöberg, translators.
Epigraph from Rumi, op cit.
Epigraph by Charles of Orleans (14 c.). *Charles of Orleans,*
1973. Sally Purcell, editor.
'my soul/the first time I saw you….' Rumi, ibid.

Point Pinos
Furthest extent of the Monterey Peninsula in California.

Map of Point Pinos - "U.S. Coast Survey, Sketch J. No.4. Indicating sites for a Light-house, 1851."

Call
Epigraph from Garcia Lorca's "Your Childhood in Menton" from *Selected Poems*, 1955. Edwin Honig, translator.

The Hidden
Epigraph paraphrased from Ramon Lull's *Book of the Lover and the Beloved*, 1954. E. Allison Peers, translator.

Aftershocks *(after Ibn Arabi)*
Based on literals by R.A. Nicholson, op. cit.
Muhyddin Ibn al'Arabi (587-662 AH/1165-1240 CE)
Sheikh al-Akbar, Sufi philosopher and poet. Crafting these versions "coincided" with living in San Francisco during the '89 earthquake, then on to Monterey. Cars for camels in these renderings. Forgive my wanderings great sheikh!

Orb Music
Epigraph from Dante Alighieri's "Paradiso" from *Divine Comedy*, 1860. H.W. Longfellow, translator.

Goddess Poems
Epigraph from ancient Greek poet Alkman, in *Three Lyric Poets of the Late Bronze Age*, 1980. Guy Davenport, translator. Epigraph from *Love Poems of Ancient Egypt*, 1960. Ezra Pound and Noel Stock, translators.

A Table at Florian's
Florian's - an 18th century cafe facing San Marco Piazza in Venice.

Martyr of Baghdad
Mansur al-Hallaj, Sufi mystic and poet (d.309 AH/913 CE). Condemned as a heretic, his body burnt to prevent resurrection. Legend notes that his ashes cried out *an'l haq* (I am the Truth) the utterance that led to his demise.

Way of the Dead
Alyscamps: Late Roman/Medieval cemetery where Gauguin
(and Van Gogh) painted.

Cardona
A promontory castle and village in Catalunya (Catalonia,
Spain). Favorite early music singer Monserrat Figueras
(with Jordi Savall and ensemble Hysperion) recorded in the
chapel of the castle.

Autumnal
Sangres: Sangre de Cristo Mountains of New Mexico.

The Last Visit
With Edwin Honig (1919–2011) poet, translator, mentor
in both, teacher and friend.

A Local Variant of Rimbaud's *Voyelles*
Arthur Rimbaud's depiction of the unity of the senses.
Sound and color become equivalent through the vowels.
This is my local, northern New Mexico version.
Kachina (katsina): Hopi/Pueblan spirit-being.

On a Fragment by Novalis
Italics by Novalis (Friedrich von Hartenberg, 1772–1801),
German poet and mystic. "From the Hidden Worlds" in
Pollen and Fragments, 1989. Arthur Versluis, translator.
trilobite: Cambrian Era (450 MYA) arthropod, first
creature to evolve an eye.

Somnambulant Ballad
Title shared with the otherwise unrelated "Romance
sonambulo" by Lorca.
"200,000 gone..." over 700 thousand a year later.
Breonna: Breonna Taylor perished in a police raid in
Louisville, sparking Black Lives Matter protests for justice.

Migrant Words
Cain was exiled to the land of Nod. And a nod to W.B. Yeats, for "deep heart's core."

Coda
See *Rumi; Poet and Mystic*. CXVIII. R.A. Nicholson, 1950.

David Cloutier grew up in New England. He pursued creative and cultural studies and graduated from Brown University with an M.A. in Creative Writing. Always a poet, he has worked as a teacher, literary publisher, arts council director, and festival producer in California, New Mexico, North Carolina and Rhode Island. Notably, he created and directed the Monterey World Music Festival (1997–2003), in an effort to expand global cultural awareness. He has translated poems by several 20th century French poets including Jean Laude and Claude Esteban. Additionally, in his search for poetic origins and consonances, he compiled several volumes of the oral poetry of the world. A seeker, sometimes finder, he lives in Santa Fe, New Mexico, with Carolyn Burns, psychotherapist.